Perioperative
Workbook

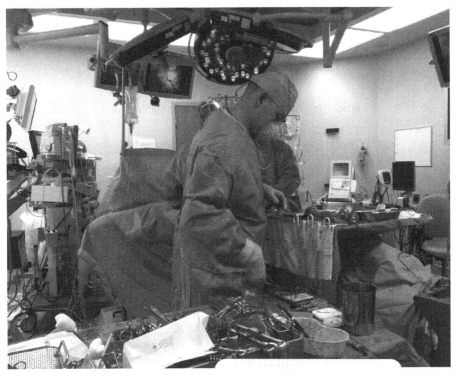

T0137509

Designed by: Ralph G Dunlap Jr.

abbott press®

A DIVISION OF WRITER'S DIGEST

Abbott Press books may be ordered through booksellers or by contacting:

Abbott Press
1663 Liberty Drive
Bloomington, IN 47403
www.abbottpress.com
Phone: 1-866-697-5310

Because of the dynamic nature of the Internet, any web addresses or links contained in this book may have changed since publication and may no longer be valid. The views expressed in this work are solely those of the author and do not necessarily reflect the views of the publisher, and the publisher hereby disclaims any responsibility for them.

Any people depicted in stock imagery provided by Thinkstock are models, and such images are being used for illustrative purposes only. Certain stock imagery © Thinkstock.

ISBN: 978-1-4582-1686-1 (sc)
ISBN: 978-1-4582-1688-5 (hc)
ISBN: 978-1-4582-1687-8 (e)

Printed in the United States of America.

Abbott Press rev. date: 06/30/2014

To The Dunlap Family

Gami and Bebe
Tina Michelle
Caiden Cole
Brooklyn Rae
Teagan Riot

Y'all mean the world to me, thanks for believing in me and
being there for me.
I love y'all
Muuuuuuuuuuuaaaaaaaaahhhhhhhh!

Table Of Contents

Introduction

My name is Ralph Dunlap Jr. I joined the United States Army As a 19 Delta Cavalry Scout in 2006. My first duty station was at FT. Hood, Texas with 3rd Armored Cavalry Regiment (3ACR). I deployed to northern Iraq for 15 Months as personal security Detachment (PSD) for the Command Sergeant Major and Colonel of 3ACR. I was injured and re-classed to a 68 Delta (Surgical Technologist). The discipline I learned as a scout prepared me to be the best at any new job I was going to take on. In 2009 I did my Phase one training at Ft. Sam Houston in San Antonio, Texas. I was told by one of my instructors that being a heart technician was being the best of the best. So hearing that, I accepted that challenge. After Graduating phase one I was shipped over to Tripler Army Medical Center (TAMC) in Honolulu, Hawaii. Tripler was where I received all of my hands on training also known as phase two in the Army. From there, my first duty station as a surgical technologist was at Brooke Army Medical Center (BAMC) in San Antonio, Texas. I can remember my very first case by myself, an emergency craniotomy on December 25th 2009. I worked at BAMC until July 2012, then to only end back up at TAMC. So, here I am today as the lead heart technologist at TAMC. I wanted to make this book so that it can be easier and more helpful for every surgical technologist and nurse out there. No matter your skill level this book will keep even the most seasoned perioperative professional organized.

Part One:
Staff Members and Contact Information

Service:_____

Surgeons: Number:	Glove size:	Contact
_____	_____	( ) -
_____	_____	( ) -
_____	_____	( ) -
_____	_____	( ) -
_____	_____	( ) -

Anesthesiologist:

_____	_____	( ) -
_____	_____	( ) -
_____	_____	( ) -

Physicians Assistant:

_____	_____	( ) -
_____	_____	( ) -

Nurses:

_____	_____	( ) -
_____	_____	( ) -
_____	_____	( ) -
_____	_____	( ) -
_____	_____	( ) -

Surgical Technologist:

_____	_____	( ) -
_____	_____	( ) -
_____	_____	( ) -
_____	_____	( ) -

ON CALL PAGERS
Anesthesiologist   (   )   -
Nurse   (   )   -
Surgical Tech   (   )   -

Service: _____

Surgeons: **Number:**	**Glove size:**	**Contact**
_____	_____	( ) -
_____	_____	( ) -
_____	_____	( ) -
_____	_____	( ) -
_____	_____	( ) -

Anesthesiologist:

_____	_____	( ) -
_____	_____	( ) -
_____	_____	( ) -

Physicians Assistant:

_____	_____	( ) -
_____	_____	( ) -

Nurses:

_____	_____	( ) -
_____	_____	( ) -
_____	_____	( ) -
_____	_____	( ) -
_____	_____	( ) -

Surgical Technologist:

_____	_____	( ) -
_____	_____	( ) -
_____	_____	( ) -
_____	_____	( ) -

ON CALL PAGERS
Anesthesiologist ( ) -
Nurse ( ) -
Surgical Tech ( ) -

Service: _____

| **Surgeons:** | **Glove size:** | **Contact** |
| **Number:** | | |

Surgeons:

_____   _____   ( ) -
_____   _____   ( ) -
_____   _____   ( ) -
_____   _____   ( ) -
_____   _____   ( ) -

Anesthesiologist:

_____   _____   ( ) -
_____   _____   ( ) -
_____   _____   ( ) -

Physicians Assistant:

_____   _____   ( ) -
_____   _____   ( ) -

Nurses:

_____   _____   ( ) -
_____   _____   ( ) -
_____   _____   ( ) -
_____   _____   ( ) -
_____   _____   ( ) -

Surgical Technologist:

_____   _____   ( ) -
_____   _____   ( ) -
_____   _____   ( ) -
_____   _____   ( ) -

ON CALL PAGERS

Anesthesiologist   ( )   -
Nurse   ( )   -
Surgical Tech   ( )   -

9

Service: _____

Surgeons: **Number:**	**Glove size:**	**Contact**
_____	_____	( ) -
_____	_____	( ) -
_____	_____	( ) -
_____	_____	( ) -
_____	_____	( ) -

Anesthesiologist:

_____	_____	( ) -
_____	_____	( ) -
_____	_____	( ) -

Physicians Assistant:

_____	_____	( ) -
_____	_____	( ) -

Nurses:

_____	_____	( ) -
_____	_____	( ) -
_____	_____	( ) -
_____	_____	( ) -
_____	_____	( ) -

Surgical Technologist:

_____	_____	( ) -
_____	_____	( ) -
_____	_____	( ) -
_____	_____	( ) -

ON CALL PAGERS

Anesthesiologist ( ) -
Nurse ( ) -
Surgical Tech ( ) -

Service: _____

Surgeons: **Number:**	**Glove size:**	**Contact**

Surgeons:
Number:

_____   _____   ( ) -
_____   _____   ( ) -
_____   _____   ( ) -
_____   _____   ( ) -
_____   _____   ( ) -

Anesthesiologist:

_____   _____   ( ) -
_____   _____   ( ) -
_____   _____   ( ) -

Physicians Assistant:

_____   _____   ( ) -
_____   _____   ( ) -

Nurses:

_____   _____   ( ) -
_____   _____   ( ) -
_____   _____   ( ) -
_____   _____   ( ) -
_____   _____   ( ) -

Surgical Technologist:

_____   _____   ( ) -
_____   _____   ( ) -
_____   _____   ( ) -
_____   _____   ( ) -

ON CALL PAGERS

Anesthesiologist ( ) -
Nurse ( ) -
Surgical Tech ( ) -

11

Service: _____

Surgeons: **Number:**	**Glove size:**	**Contact**
_____	_____	( ) -
_____	_____	( ) -
_____	_____	( ) -
_____	_____	( ) -
_____	_____	( ) -

Anesthesiologist:

_____	_____	( ) -
_____	_____	( ) -
_____	_____	( ) -

Physicians Assistant:

_____	_____	( ) -
_____	_____	( ) -

Nurses:

_____	_____	( ) -
_____	_____	( ) -
_____	_____	( ) -
_____	_____	( ) -
_____	_____	( ) -

Surgical Technologist:

_____	_____	( ) -
_____	_____	( ) -
_____	_____	( ) -
_____	_____	( ) -

ON CALL PAGERS
Anesthesiologist ( ) -
Nurse ( ) -
Surgical Tech ( ) -

Part Two:
Medical Rep Contact Information

Medical Rep Information

Name	Rep Company	Contact Number
_____	_____	(___) ___ - ___
_____	_____	(___) ___ - ___
_____	_____	(___) ___ - ___
_____	_____	(___) ___ - ___
_____	_____	(___) ___ - ___
_____	_____	(___) ___ - ___
_____	_____	(___) ___ - ___
_____	_____	(___) ___ - ___
_____	_____	(___) ___ - ___
_____	_____	(___) ___ - ___
_____	_____	(___) ___ - ___
_____	_____	(___) ___ - ___
_____	_____	(___) ___ - ___
_____	_____	(___) ___ - ___
_____	_____	(___) ___ - ___
_____	_____	(___) ___ - ___
_____	_____	(___) ___ - ___
_____	_____	(___) ___ - ___
_____	_____	(___) ___ - ___
_____	_____	(___) ___ - ___
_____	_____	(___) ___ - ___
_____	_____	(___) ___ - ___
_____	_____	(___) ___ - ___
_____	_____	(___) ___ - ___
_____	_____	(___) ___ - ___
_____	_____	(___) ___ - ___
_____	_____	(___) ___ - ___
_____	_____	(___) ___ - ___

Notes:

_____

_____

_____

Name	Rep Company	Contact Number
_____	_____	( ) -
_____	_____	( ) -
_____	_____	( ) -
_____	_____	( ) -
_____	_____	( ) -
_____	_____	( ) -
_____	_____	( ) -
_____	_____	( ) -
_____	_____	( ) -
_____	_____	( ) -
_____	_____	( ) -
_____	_____	( ) -
_____	_____	( ) -
_____	_____	( ) -
_____	_____	( ) -
_____	_____	( ) -
_____	_____	( ) -
_____	_____	( ) -
_____	_____	( ) -
_____	_____	( ) -
_____	_____	( ) -
_____	_____	( ) -
_____	_____	( ) -
_____	_____	( ) -
_____	_____	( ) -
_____	_____	( ) -
_____	_____	( ) -
_____	_____	( ) -
_____	_____	( ) -
_____	_____	( ) -
_____	_____	( ) -
_____	_____	( ) -

Notes:

_____

_____

_____

Medical Rep Business Cards

Part Three:
Procedures/Preference Cards/Room Set Up

Room Setup:

-
-
-
-
-
-
-
-
-
-

Important Notes:

Back Table Notes:

-
-
-
-
-
-
-
-
-
-

Important Notes:

Instruments

- _____
- _____
- _____
- _____
- _____
- _____
- _____
- _____
- _____
- _____
- _____
- _____

Pull Bucket

Suture

_____	_____
_____	_____
_____	_____
_____	_____
_____	_____
_____	_____
_____	_____
_____	_____
_____	_____
_____	_____
_____	_____
_____	_____

Pull Bucket

_____

(Procedure)

Head of
OR BED

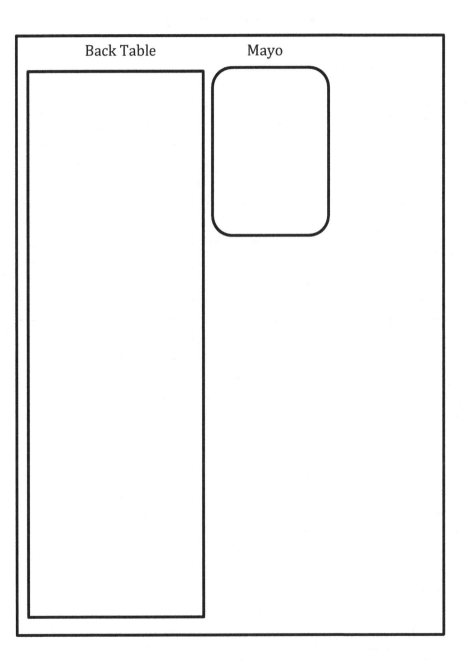

Back Table   Mayo

Procedure Outline

Room Setup:

-
-
-
-
-
-
-
-
-
-

Important Notes:

Back Table Notes:

-
-
-
-
-
-
-
-
-
-

Important Notes:

Instruments

- _____
- _____
- _____
- _____
- _____
- _____
- _____
- _____
- _____
- _____
- _____

Pull Bucket

Suture

_____	_____
_____	_____
_____	_____
_____	_____
_____	_____
_____	_____
_____	_____
_____	_____
_____	_____
_____	_____
_____	_____
_____	_____

Pull Bucket

_____

Head of
OR BED

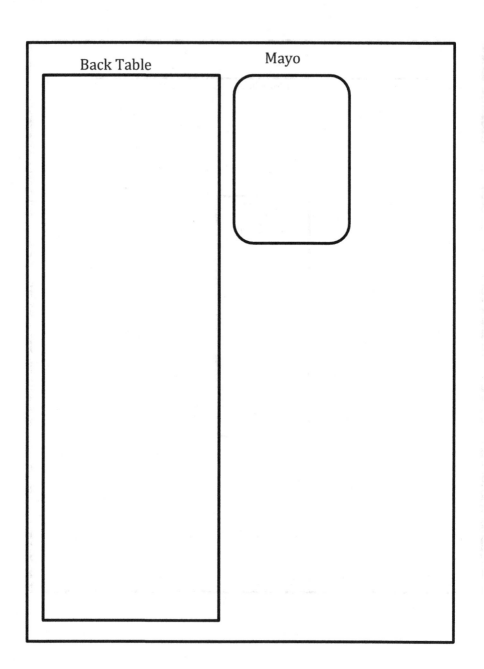

Back Table

Mayo

Procedure Outline

_____
_____
_____
_____
_____
_____
_____
_____
_____
_____
_____
_____
_____
_____
_____
_____
_____
_____
_____
_____
_____
_____
_____
_____
_____
_____
_____
_____
_____
_____
_____

Room Setup:

-
-
-
-
-
-
-
-
-

Important Notes:

Back Table Notes:

-
-
-
-
-
-
-
-
-

Important Notes:

Instruments

- _____
- _____
- _____
- _____
- _____
- _____
- _____
- _____
- _____
- _____
- _____
- _____

Pull Bucket

Suture

_____   _____

_____   _____

_____   _____

_____   _____

_____   _____

_____   _____

_____   _____

_____   _____

_____   _____

_____   _____

_____   _____

Pull Bucket

Head of
OR BED

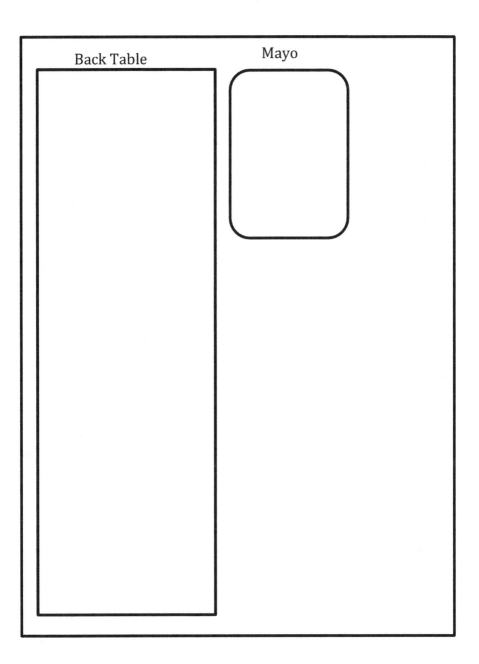

Back Table

Mayo

Procedure Outline

Room Setup:

-
-
-
-
-
-
-
-
-
-

Important Notes:

Back Table Notes:

-
-
-
-
-
-
-
-
-
-

Important Notes:

Instruments

- _____
- _____
- _____
- _____
- _____
- _____
- _____
- _____
- _____
- _____
- _____
- _____

Pull Bucket

Suture

_____ _____
_____ _____
_____ _____
_____ _____
_____ _____
_____ _____
_____ _____
_____ _____
_____ _____
_____ _____
_____ _____

Pull Bucket

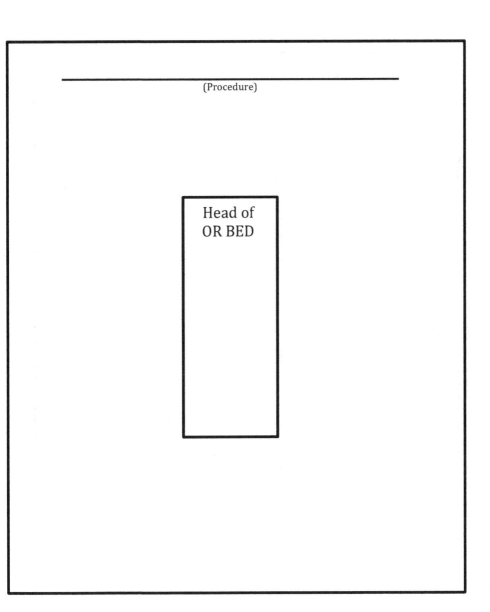

_____
(Procedure)

Head of
OR BED

53

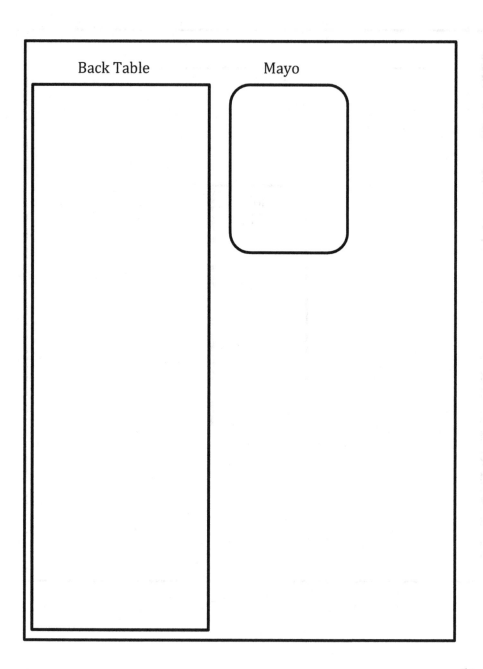

Back Table

Mayo

Procedure Outline

_____

_____

_____

_____

_____

_____

_____

_____

_____

_____

_____

_____

_____

_____

_____

_____

_____

_____

_____

_____

_____

_____

_____

_____

_____

_____

_____

_____

Room Setup:

-
-
-
-
-
-
-
-
-
-

Important Notes:

Back Table Notes:

-
-
-
-
-
-
-
-
-

Important Notes:

Instruments

- _____
- _____
- _____
- _____
- _____
- _____
- _____
- _____
- _____
- _____
- _____
- _____

Pull Bucket

Suture

_____   _____

_____   _____

_____   _____

_____   _____

_____   _____

_____   _____

_____   _____

_____   _____

_____   _____

_____   _____

Pull Bucket

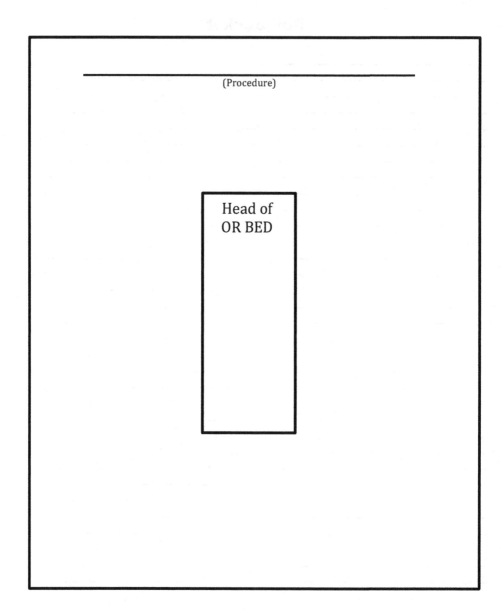

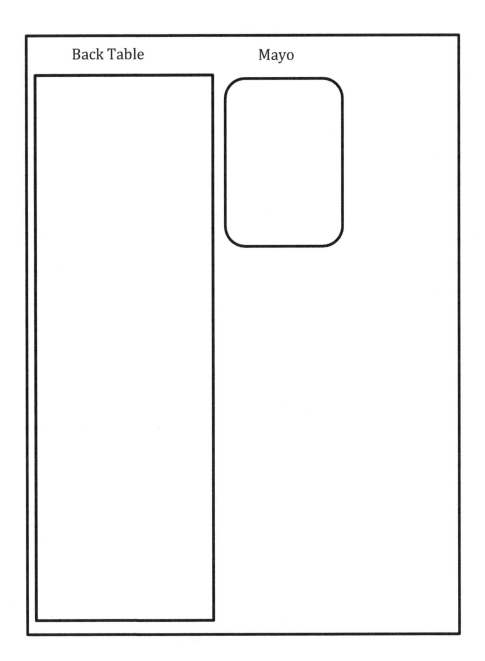

Back Table

Mayo

Procedure Outline

Room Setup:

-
-
-
-
-
-
-
-
-
-

Important Notes:

Back Table Notes:

-
-
-
-
-
-
-
-
-
-

Important Notes:

Instruments

- _____
- _____
- _____
- _____
- _____
- _____
- _____
- _____
- _____
- _____
- _____

Pull Bucket

Suture

_____   _____
_____   _____
_____   _____
_____   _____
_____   _____
_____   _____
_____   _____
_____   _____
_____   _____
_____   _____
_____   _____

Pull Bucket

_____

(Procedure)

```
┌─────────────┐
│ Head of     │
│ OR BED      │
│             │
│             │
│             │
│             │
└─────────────┘
```

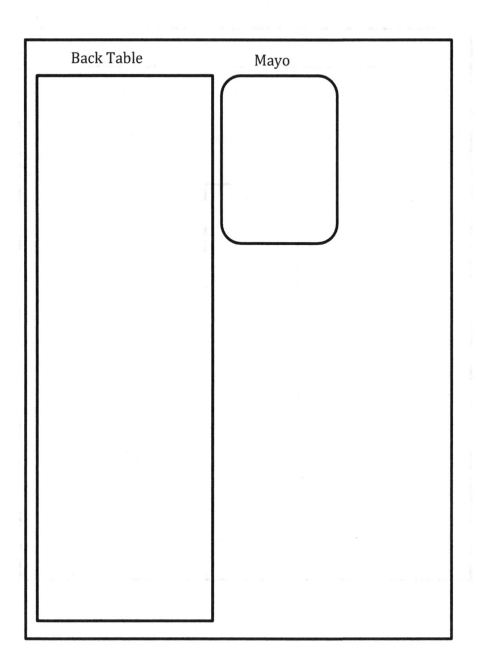

Back Table

Mayo

72

Procedure Outline

Room Setup:

-
-
-
-
-
-
-
-
-
-

Important Notes:

Back Table Notes:

-
-
-
-
-
-
-
-
-

Important Notes:

Instruments

- _____
- _____
- _____
- _____
- _____
- _____
- _____
- _____
- _____
- _____
- _____
- _____

Pull Bucket

Suture

_____   _____
_____   _____
_____   _____
_____   _____
_____   _____
_____   _____
_____   _____
_____   _____
_____   _____
_____   _____

Pull Bucket

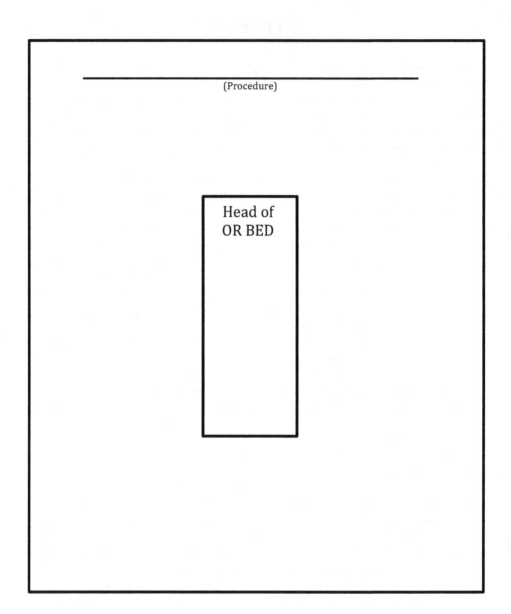

(Procedure)

Head of
OR BED

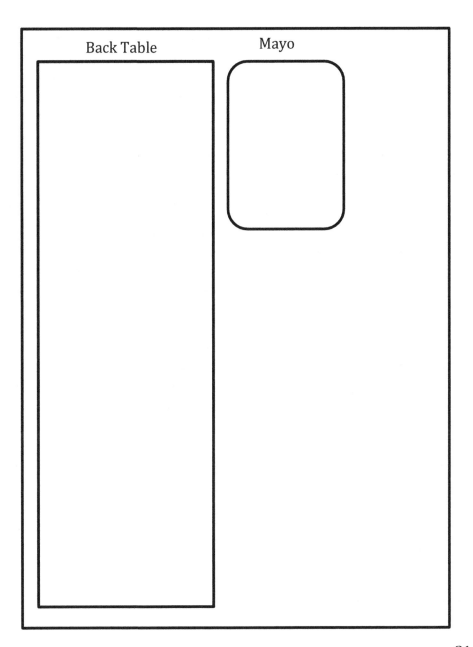

Back Table

Mayo

Procedure Outline

_____
_____
_____
_____
_____
_____
_____
_____
_____
_____
_____
_____
_____
_____
_____
_____
_____
_____
_____
_____
_____
_____
_____
_____
_____
_____
_____

Room Setup:

-
-
-
-
-
-
-
-
-
-

Important Notes:

Back Table Notes:

-
-
-
-
-
-
-
-
-
-

Important Notes:

Instruments

- _____
- _____
- _____
- _____
- _____
- _____
- _____
- _____
- _____
- _____
- _____
- _____

Pull Bucket

Suture

_____   _____
_____   _____
_____   _____
_____   _____
_____   _____
_____   _____
_____   _____
_____   _____
_____   _____
_____   _____
_____   _____
_____   _____

Pull Bucket

_____
(Procedure)

Head of
OR BED

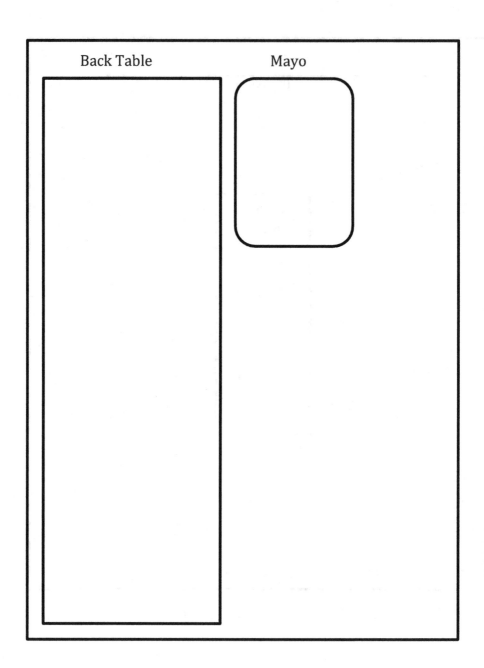

Back Table

Mayo

Procedure Outline

_____

_____

_____

_____

_____

_____

_____

_____

_____

_____

_____

_____

_____

_____

_____

_____

_____

_____

_____

_____

_____

_____

_____

_____

_____

_____

_____

_____

_____

Room Setup:

-
-
-
-
-
-
-
-
-
-

Important Notes:

Back Table Notes:

-
-
-
-
-
-
-
-
-

Important Notes:

Instruments

- _____
- _____
- _____
- _____
- _____
- _____
- _____
- _____
- _____
- _____
- _____
- _____

Pull Bucket

Suture

_____   _____
_____   _____
_____   _____
_____   _____
_____   _____
_____   _____
_____   _____
_____   _____
_____   _____
_____   _____
_____   _____

Pull Bucket

_____

Head of
OR BED

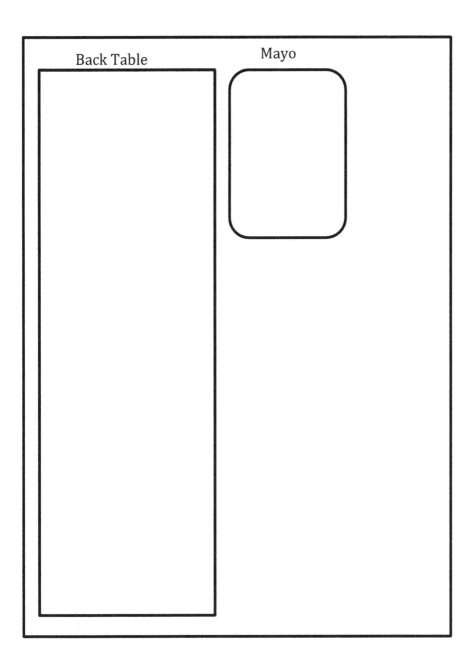

Back Table

Mayo

Procedure Outline

_____
_____
_____
_____
_____
_____
_____
_____
_____
_____
_____
_____
_____
_____
_____
_____
_____
_____
_____
_____
_____
_____
_____
_____
_____
_____
_____
_____
_____
_____

(Procedure)

Room Setup:

-
-
-
-
-
-
-
-
-
-

Important Notes:

Back Table Notes:

-
-
-
-
-
-
-
-
-
-

Important Notes:

Instruments

- _____
- _____
- _____
- _____
- _____
- _____
- _____
- _____
- _____
- _____
- _____

Pull Bucket

Suture

Pull Bucket

_____
(Procedure)

Head of
OR BED

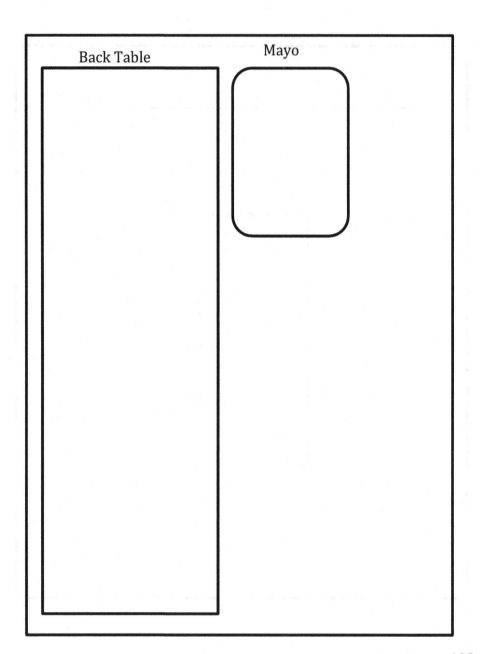

Back Table

Mayo

Procedure Outline

_____

_____

_____

_____

_____

_____

_____

_____

_____

_____

_____

_____

_____

_____

_____

_____

_____

_____

_____

_____

_____

_____

_____

_____

_____

_____

_____

_____

_____

_____

_____

_____

Part Four:
Personal Case Log /
Continuing Education
Unit Log

Case Log

Name: _____

Date Range: _____

Case #	Procedure date	Surgical Procedure	Role
_____	___/___/_____	_____	____
_____	___/___/_____	_____	____
_____	___/___/_____	_____	____
_____	___/___/_____	_____	____
_____	___/___/_____	_____	____
_____	___/___/_____	_____	____
_____	___/___/_____	_____	____
_____	___/___/_____	_____	____
_____	___/___/_____	_____	____
_____	___/___/_____	_____	____
_____	___/___/_____	_____	____
_____	___/___/_____	_____	____
_____	___/___/_____	_____	____
_____	___/___/_____	_____	____
_____	___/___/_____	_____	____
_____	___/___/_____	_____	____
_____	___/___/_____	_____	____
_____	___/___/_____	_____	____
_____	___/___/_____	_____	____
_____	___/___/_____	_____	____
_____	___/___/_____	_____	____
_____	___/___/_____	_____	____
_____	___/___/_____	_____	____
_____	___/___/_____	_____	____
_____	___/___/_____	_____	____
_____	___/___/_____	_____	____
_____	___/___/_____	_____	____
_____	___/___/_____	_____	____
_____	___/___/_____	_____	____
_____	___/___/_____	_____	____
_____	___/___/_____	_____	____
_____	___/___/_____	_____	____
_____	___/___/_____	_____	____
_____	___/___/_____	_____	____
_____	___/___/_____	_____	____
_____	___/___/_____	_____	____
_____	___/___/_____	_____	____
_____	___/___/_____	_____	____

Case #	Procedure date	Surgical Procedure	Role
_____	___/___/___	_____	____
_____	___/___/___	_____	____
_____	___/___/___	_____	____
_____	___/___/___	_____	____
_____	___/___/___	_____	____
_____	___/___/___	_____	____
_____	___/___/___	_____	____
_____	___/___/___	_____	____
_____	___/___/___	_____	____
_____	___/___/___	_____	____
_____	___/___/___	_____	____
_____	___/___/___	_____	____
_____	___/___/___	_____	____
_____	___/___/___	_____	____
_____	___/___/___	_____	____
_____	___/___/___	_____	____
_____	___/___/___	_____	____
_____	___/___/___	_____	____
_____	___/___/___	_____	____
_____	___/___/___	_____	____
_____	___/___/___	_____	____
_____	___/___/___	_____	____
_____	___/___/___	_____	____
_____	___/___/___	_____	____
_____	___/___/___	_____	____
_____	___/___/___	_____	____
_____	___/___/___	_____	____
_____	___/___/___	_____	____
_____	___/___/___	_____	____
_____	___/___/___	_____	____
_____	___/___/___	_____	____
_____	___/___/___	_____	____
_____	___/___/___	_____	____
_____	___/___/___	_____	____
_____	___/___/___	_____	____
_____	___/___/___	_____	____
_____	___/___/___	_____	____
_____	___/___/___	_____	____
_____	___/___/___	_____	____
_____	___/___/___	_____	____

Case #	Procedure date	Surgical Procedure	Role
_____	___/___/___	_____	___
_____	___/___/___	_____	___
_____	___/___/___	_____	___
_____	___/___/___	_____	___
_____	___/___/___	_____	___
_____	___/___/___	_____	___
_____	___/___/___	_____	___
_____	___/___/___	_____	___
_____	___/___/___	_____	___
_____	___/___/___	_____	___
_____	___/___/___	_____	___
_____	___/___/___	_____	___
_____	___/___/___	_____	___
_____	___/___/___	_____	___
_____	___/___/___	_____	___
_____	___/___/___	_____	___
_____	___/___/___	_____	___
_____	___/___/___	_____	___
_____	___/___/___	_____	___
_____	___/___/___	_____	___
_____	___/___/___	_____	___
_____	___/___/___	_____	___
_____	___/___/___	_____	___
_____	___/___/___	_____	___
_____	___/___/___	_____	___
_____	___/___/___	_____	___
_____	___/___/___	_____	___
_____	___/___/___	_____	___
_____	___/___/___	_____	___
_____	___/___/___	_____	___
_____	___/___/___	_____	___
_____	___/___/___	_____	___
_____	___/___/___	_____	___
_____	___/___/___	_____	___
_____	___/___/___	_____	___
_____	___/___/___	_____	___
_____	___/___/___	_____	___
_____	___/___/___	_____	___
_____	___/___/___	_____	___

Case #	Procedure date	Surgical Procedure	Role
_____	___/___/___	_____	___
_____	___/___/___	_____	___
_____	___/___/___	_____	___
_____	___/___/___	_____	___
_____	___/___/___	_____	___
_____	___/___/___	_____	___
_____	___/___/___	_____	___
_____	___/___/___	_____	___
_____	___/___/___	_____	___
_____	___/___/___	_____	___
_____	___/___/___	_____	___
_____	___/___/___	_____	___
_____	___/___/___	_____	___
_____	___/___/___	_____	___
_____	___/___/___	_____	___
_____	___/___/___	_____	___
_____	___/___/___	_____	___
_____	___/___/___	_____	___
_____	___/___/___	_____	___
_____	___/___/___	_____	___
_____	___/___/___	_____	___
_____	___/___/___	_____	___
_____	___/___/___	_____	___
_____	___/___/___	_____	___
_____	___/___/___	_____	___
_____	___/___/___	_____	___
_____	___/___/___	_____	___
_____	___/___/___	_____	___
_____	___/___/___	_____	___
_____	___/___/___	_____	___
_____	___/___/___	_____	___
_____	___/___/___	_____	___
_____	___/___/___	_____	___
_____	___/___/___	_____	___
_____	___/___/___	_____	___
_____	___/___/___	_____	___

Case #	Procedure date	Surgical Procedure	Role
_____	___/___/___	_____	____
_____	___/___/___	_____	____
_____	___/___/___	_____	____
_____	___/___/___	_____	____
_____	___/___/___	_____	____
_____	___/___/___	_____	____
_____	___/___/___	_____	____
_____	___/___/___	_____	____
_____	___/___/___	_____	____
_____	___/___/___	_____	____
_____	___/___/___	_____	____
_____	___/___/___	_____	____
_____	___/___/___	_____	____
_____	___/___/___	_____	____
_____	___/___/___	_____	____
_____	___/___/___	_____	____
_____	___/___/___	_____	____
_____	___/___/___	_____	____
_____	___/___/___	_____	____
_____	___/___/___	_____	____
_____	___/___/___	_____	____
_____	___/___/___	_____	____
_____	___/___/___	_____	____
_____	___/___/___	_____	____
_____	___/___/___	_____	____
_____	___/___/___	_____	____
_____	___/___/___	_____	____
_____	___/___/___	_____	____
_____	___/___/___	_____	____
_____	___/___/___	_____	____
_____	___/___/___	_____	____
_____	___/___/___	_____	____
_____	___/___/___	_____	____
_____	___/___/___	_____	____
_____	___/___/___	_____	____
_____	___/___/___	_____	____
_____	___/___/___	_____	____
_____	___/___/___	_____	____

Continuing Education Units Log

Date	Name Of Course	Hours
___/___/_____	_____	_____
___/___/_____	_____	_____
___/___/_____	_____	_____
___/___/_____	_____	_____
___/___/_____	_____	_____
___/___/_____	_____	_____
___/___/_____	_____	_____
___/___/_____	_____	_____
___/___/_____	_____	_____
___/___/_____	_____	_____
___/___/_____	_____	_____
___/___/_____	_____	_____
___/___/_____	_____	_____
___/___/_____	_____	_____
___/___/_____	_____	_____
___/___/_____	_____	_____
___/___/_____	_____	_____
___/___/_____	_____	_____
___/___/_____	_____	_____
___/___/_____	_____	_____
___/___/_____	_____	_____
___/___/_____	_____	_____
___/___/_____	_____	_____
___/___/_____	_____	_____
___/___/_____	_____	_____
___/___/_____	_____	_____
___/___/_____	_____	_____
___/___/_____	_____	_____
___/___/_____	_____	_____
___/___/_____	_____	_____
___/___/_____	_____	_____
___/___/_____	_____	_____
___/___/_____	_____	_____
___/___/_____	_____	_____
___/___/_____	_____	_____
___/___/_____	_____	_____
___/___/_____	_____	_____
___/___/_____	_____	_____

Part Five:
Personal Notes / Surgical Terms

NOTES:

Medical Prefixes and Suffixes

PREFIXES

A-/An-	not, without, less, absent
Ab-	Away from, off
Ad-	To, toward
Aer-	Air
Amb-	Both, on both sides
Amph-	On both sides
Angio-	To do with arteries
Ante-	Before
Anti-	Against, opposite
Apo-	From, opposed
Auto-	Self
Bi-	Twice, double
Brachy-	Short
Brady-	Slow
Cardio-	The heart
Cata-	Down, back, apart
Cephal-	The head
Chole-	To do with bile
Chromo-	Colour
Circum-	Around
Colo-	To do with the colon
Con-	Together
Cyan-	Blue
Contra-	Against
Cyst-	Bag, bladder
Cyto-	Cell
Dacry-	Tears
Dactyl-	Finger or toe
De-	From, not
Deci-	Tenth
Demi-	Half
Dent-	Teeth

Derma-	Skin
Di-	Two, twice, double
Dia-	Through, across
Diplo-	Double
Dis-	Apart, absence of
Docho-	Relating to a duct
Dys-	Bad or abnormal
Ect-, Ecto-	External, outside
Eu-	Normal
Endo-	In, within, inside
Entero-	Small intestine
Epi-	On, over, above
Ex, exo-	Out
Extra-	Beyond or outside
Fore-	Before, in front of
Galacto-	Milk
Gastro-	The stomach
Genic-	Producing or related to genes
Glosso-	The tongue
Haem-	Blood
Hemi-	Half, partial
Hepato-	Liver
Hetero-	Other, dissimilar
Holo-	All
Homo-	Same, similar
Hydro-	Water or liquid
Hyper-	Above or excessive
Hypo-	Under or low
Idio-	Private or individual
Ileo-	The ileum
Infra-	Beneath
Inter-	Between, among
Intra-	Within or inside
Intro-	Into or inward
Iso-	Equal
Juxtra-	Near
Kerato-	Horn-like tissue, cornea
Kinese-	Movement
Lact-	Milk
Laparo-	Abdomen, loin
Laryngo-	Larynx
Latero-	Side
Lepto-	Thin, light, frail
Leuko-	White

Litho-	Stone or callculus
Macro-	Large
Mal-	Bad
Medi-	Middle
Mega-	Large
Melano-	Black
Meno-	Menopause
Meso-	Middle, intermediate
Meta-	Later, behind
Micro-	Small
Mio-	Less, smaller
Mono-	Single
Multi-	Many
Myco-	Fungus, fungi
Myo-	Muscle
Myelo-	Marrow
Myxo-	Mucus
Neo-	New, recent
Nephro-	Kidney
Neuro-	Nerves
Non-	No
Ob-	Against
Oculo-	Eye
Odont-	Tooth
Oligo-	Few
Omo-	Shoulder
Oo-	Ovum, egg
Opisth-	Backward
Orchid-	Testicle
Ortho-	Correct; straight
Os-	Mouth, bone
Osteo-	Bone
Oxy-	Sharp
Pachy-	Thick
Pan-	All
Para-	Beside, faulty
Path-	Disease
Per-	Going through a structure
Peri-	Around
Pleo-	More
Pneu-, Pneumo-	Lungs, breathing
Pod-	Foot
Poikilo-	Iregular, varied

Poly-	More than one
Post-	After
Pre-	Before
Pro-	Before
Procto-	Anus, rectum
Proto-	First
Pseudo-	False, spurious
Psych-	Mind
Py-	Pus
Pyelo-	Relating to the pelvis of the kidney
Re-	Again
Retro-	Backward
Rhino-	Nose, nasal
Sacro-	Sacrum
Salpingo-	Fallopian tube
Sarco-	Flesh
Sclero-	Hard
Scoto-	Darkness
Somato-	Relating to the body
Steato-	Fat
Stetho-	Chest
Sub-	Under, below, beneath
Supra-	Over, on top of
Syn-	With, together
Tachy-	Accelerated, rapid
Tampon-	To plug
Thermo-	Heat
Thyro-	Thyroid
Trans-	Going across a structure
Tropho-	Nourishment, nutrition
Uni-	One, single
Uro-	Urine
Vaso-	A vessel
Verm-	Worm-like
Xanth-	Yellow

SUFFIXES

-aceous	Resembling
-ade	An action
-aemia	Blood
-aesthes	Sensation
-agogue	Substance promoting a flow of something
-algia	Pain
-cardial	Relating to the heart
-cele	Tumor, cyst, hernia
-cephalic	Head
-cide	Causing death
-coel(e)	A cavity
-cyst	A fluid filled sac
-cyte	Cell e.g. phagocyte
-creas	Flesh
-dynia	Pain
-ectasia	Dilatation of ducts
-ectomy	Surgical excision of a part of the body
-fuge	To drive away
-genic	The capacity to produce
-gogue	To make flow
-gram	An imaging technique using contrast medium
-itis	Inflammation
-lasis	Condition, pathological state
-lysis	Set free, disintegrate
-megaly	Abnormal enlargement
-morphic	Something that has a particular form, shape, or structure
-nexal	From 'nexus' indicating a connection or link
-oid	Shape, resemblance
-oma	A tumor
-osis	Abnormal condition, process
-oscopy	Inspection of a cavity
-ostomy	A connection between two hollow organs
-ostosis	Formation of bone
-otomy	To cut into a part of the body
-penia	Lack
-phagia	Eating
-pathy	Disorder or disease
-plasia	Growth or formation
-plasty	Surgical revision

-plegia	Paralysis
-pnoea	Breath, respiration
-poiesis	Production
-rhage	Flow
-rhaphy	Suturing
-rrhoea	Flow, discharge
-sclerosis	Dryness, hardness
-scopy	To see
-stomosis	To create an outlet
-systole	Contraction of the heart
-tomy	Cutting
-trophic	Nourishment
-tropic	Having an affinity for, turning towards
-uretic	To do with urine

Part Six:
Examples

Coronary Artery Bypass Graft

- **Room Setup:**
- Blanket warmer underneath the megadyne pad
- Long sheet on top of Megadyne pad to tuck the Pt. arms
- Bovie at the foot of the bed
- 2nd bovie with defibrillator at the head of the bed
- Extra mayo stand for anesthesia to do central line
- Floor mats on both sides of the bed
- Stool on right side of patient for surgeon to take down the mammary

- **Important Notes:**
- Remember to move the bed down so that there is enough room for the tech and surgeon to work comfortably. Make sure we have the right table.

- **Back Table Notes:**
- If off pump don't forget to make spooner sponge
- Set up vein harvest set for the Physician Assistant
- Have CABG solution in 3cc syringe, specimen cup with raytec
- Have a separate bowl with CABG solution for graft
- Extra 11 blade for PA
- 3mm super sharp for poking the coronary arteries

- **Important Notes:**
  _____
  _____
  _____
  _____
  _____
  _____
  _____

CABG OFF PUMP

Instruments

- Open Heart Pack
- Stryker Sternal Saw (Short Saw Guide)
- Sternal Saw and Retractor Set (Retractors Only)
- Medtronic Off Pump Retractor Set
- Rultract IMA Retractor Set
- Adult Defib Pads
- Open Heart Set
- Open Heart Accessories
- CT Scanlan Set
- Horizon Clip Appliers
- Vein Harvest Set
- HD Storz Camera
- Guidant Scope
- Sterile Mayo Stand Trey
- Sterile Metal Basin
- Sterile Drape Sheets x2

Pull Bucket

Suture

6-0 Prolene C-1	x 3 (Proximals)		2-0 Cardiac Pacing Wire	x 4
7-0 Prolene BV-1	x 3 (Distals)		5-0 Silk RB-1	x 2
7-0 Prolene BV-1.75	x 1 (Mammary)		0 Silk SH (Spooner Sponge)	x 1
0 Silk CT-2 Cr/8	x 2 (Pericardial)			

Closing Suture

0 Vicryl CT-1	x 2	4-0 Monocryl PS-2	x 3
2-0 Vicryl SH	x 1		
2-0 Vicryl CT-1	x 2		

Pull Bucket

Sternal Saw Blade

Cell Saver Tubing

Vein Cannula

Insulflation Tubing

Horizon Clips Small x 12

Horizon Clips Large x 2

Pledgets

Mister Blower

3cc Syringe

Octopus (Heart Holder)

4 x 10 OP Sites

#11 Blade (For Vein Harvest Set)

Medtronic Octobase

Aortic Punch 4.0

1:2 Blake Connector

Warming Drape W/ Slush

Horizon Clips Medium x 6

24 Guage Angio Catheter

Surgicel 3 x 6

19 Fr Blake Drains x 2

Bath Towels x 2

VasoView HemoPro 2

3mm Super Blade

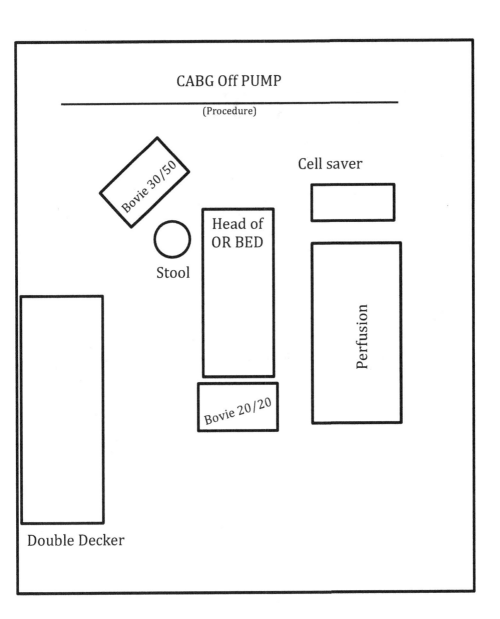

CABG Off PUMP

(Procedure)

Bovie 30/50

Cell saver

Stool

Head of
OR BED

Perfusion

Bovie 20/20

Double Decker

CABG

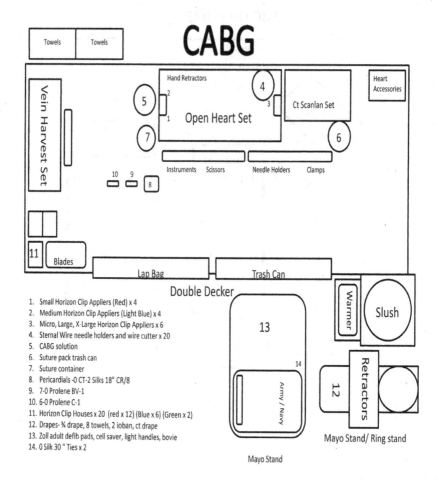

Towels	Towels	

Vein Harvest Set

Hand Retractors

5
2
1
Open Heart Set
4
3
7

Ct Scanlan Set

Heart Accessories

6

Instruments   Scissors   Needle Holders   Clamps

10   9
8

11   Blades

Lap Bag   Trash Can

Double Decker

Warmer

Slush

13

14

Army / Navy

Retractors

12

Mayo Stand

Mayo Stand/ Ring stand

1. Small Horizon Clip Appliers (Red) x 4
2. Medium Horizon Clip Appliers (Light Blue) x 4
3. Micro, Large, X-Large Horizon Clip Appliers x 6
4. Sternal Wire needle holders and wire cutter x 20
5. CABG solution
6. Suture pack trash can
7. Suture container
8. Pericardials -0 CT-2 Silks 18" CR/8
9. 7-0 Prolene BV-1
10. 6-0 Prolene C-1
11. Horizon Clip Houses x 20 (red x 12) (Blue x 6) (Green x 2)
12. Drapes- ¾ drape, 8 towels, 2 ioban, ct drape
13. Zoll adult defib pads, cell saver, light handles, bovie
14. 0 Silk 30 " Ties x 2

Step-By-Step Off-Pump CABG

1. **DRAPING**

   ¾ Sheet
   Groin Towel- folded in thirds lengthwise
   Towels for the feet x 2 with PTC
   Blue towels to drape body x 6
   Ioban x 2
   CV Drape sheet
   Adult Defib Internal Paddles
   Bovie w/ Teflon tip
   Cell Saver tubing

2. **OPENING THE CHEST**

   # 10 blade
   Bovie with Teflon tip
   Army/Navy retractor
   Stryker Sternal Saw (blade always up)
   Rake retractors x 2
   The Doctor will now stop all bleeders might ask for Flo-Seal 10 mL

3. **TAKING THE IMA (Internal Mammary Artery**

   10" Angled DeBakey's (Dr. Verghese)
   6" Gerald Forceps (Dr. Stockmaster)
   Bovie
   Horizon Clips – Small and Medium
   Tenotomy scissors
   Metz
   Gerald Forceps or Mills to open up the artery
   CABG 3 mL syringe
   CABG soaked Ray-tec
   Bulldog

4. **OPENING AND RETRACTING THE PERICARDIUM**

   Laps folded in half x 2
   Sternal retractor
   Bovie
   Heavy 7" DeBakey's
   "Pericardials" 0-Silk CT-2 Pop-Offs

5. MAKING THE GRAFT SITE

This is where you bring up the Coronary set up trey:
6 forceps Geralds, Mills, DeBakey all three fine tip forceps (BLUE)
Beaver blade
Beaver blade with Super Sharp
Forward Potts
Reverse Potts
> The steps for these instruments are
> 1. Beaver Blade
> 2. Super Sharp
> 3. Forward Potts
> 4. Reverse Potts
> 5. Then after the last cut with the reverse the surgeon will ask for a shunt they range from 1.0 - 3.0. The Nurse will open the shunt when asked for it.

6. ATTACHING THE DISTAL ASPECT OF THE GRAFT

Bring up the vein graft that has been pulled from the leg
Right after they do the reverse potts and the shunt
The GOOD 7-0 Prolene BV-1.75 for IMA ony with a SHOT on the other needle
Then they will do the distals and ask for a 7-0 Prolene BV-1 with a shot on the other needle.
When you cut and take the needles from the surgeons get ready to splash their hands with warm saline.
Metz to cut the suture
The taking stitch which is the 5-0 silk RB-1 for tacking the IMA down

7. ATTACHING THE PROXIMAL ASPECT OF THE GRAFT

Aortic Punch with Sharp
Lap to wipe off debris from the punch
6-0 Prolene C-1 to connect the graft
All repair stitches are going to be 6-0 C-1 for Proximal

8. CHEST TUBES

#15 Blade
Fine tonsil
19 fr round Blake Drain
2:1 Y drain connector
Pericardials will be the suture to hold down the drains.

8. CLOSING THE CHEST- FROM STERNUM TO SKIN

Rakes x 2
7 Sternal wires depending on Pt. Size
Sternal wire driver on needle end and a stubby on the other end
The assistant gets an extra stubby
Wire cutter
Twister- Big sterna wire driver
Turner Downer
Irrigate with warm irrigation and two bulb syringes
Sternal Blue surgeon will pick plates and screws
Bonnies
0 Vicryl CT-2 x 2
Adsons
2-0 Vicryl CT-1 x 2
4-0 monocryl PS-2 x 2
Sloppy wet
Dry
Aquacel
4x8 dressing for chest tubes
Medipore tape to cover